Original title:
Rising from Love Lost

Author: Liina Liblikas
ISBN HARDBACK: 978-9916-89-904-5
ISBN PAPERBACK: 978-9916-89-905-2
ISBN EBOOK: 978-9916-89-951-9

Portals of Grace

In shadows deep, where mercy flows,
A light emerges, softly glows.
With humble hearts, we seek the way,
Towards grace divine, where souls can pray.

The golden gates, they swing so wide,
Revealing love that will abide.
Each step we take, in faith we tread,
Through trials faced, our spirits led.

In whispers soft, the angels call,
A sacred dance, we heed the thrall.
Transgressions washed, in waters pure,
Through open doors, our path is sure.

Through storms of life, both fierce and frail,
The heart finds peace; it will not fail.
With every breath, a prayer we share,
In portals wide, we find our care.

In unity, we rise and sing,
Of joyous hope that faith can bring.
Beneath the skies, in love we trace,
The holy bonds of God's embrace.

Resurrection of the Forgotten

In shadows deep, they whispered low,
The souls long gone, a silent woe.
But with the dawn, their voices rise,
Awakening hope beneath the skies.

From ashes pale, their dreams reborn,
The light of grace, bright as the morn.
Through trials faced, with faith they stand,
To seek the truth, a guiding hand.

Each heart a vessel, cast to sea,
In every tear, a drop of plea.
The forgotten rise, with spirits strong,
Their hymn of love, an endless song.

In sacred space, where mercy flows,
They gather close, as kindness grows.
For every wound, a healer's touch,
In unity's heart, we find so much.

Resurrection blooms with each new day,
As light dispels the night away.
In joyful cries, we find our place,
Together, we stride in endless grace.

Seraphim's Embrace

In the heavens bright, they take their flight,
Seraphim dance in eternal light.
Wings of fire, hearts ablaze,
They sing of love in endless praise.

A whisper soft, through time it weaves,
The sacred bond that never leaves.
With eyes like stars, they gaze below,
Guiding souls through joy and woe.

In the stillness, their warmth we feel,
With every prayer, our spirits heal.
They guard our dreams as shadows sway,
In gentle light, they show the way.

With arms outstretched, they hold us near,
In the darkest hour, conquering fear.
An embrace divine, forever true,
In seraphim's grace, we are renewed.

To the highest throne, we lift our song,
In sacred trust, we all belong.
For love that binds, we rise above,
In seraphim's embrace, we find our love.

Elysian Light after the Fall

Once shadows dwelt in Eden's grace,
A world of hope, a sacred space.
Yet darkness crept, the heart turned cold,
A tale of sorrow, lost and old.

But from the ruins, light will bloom,
Restoring life, dispelling gloom.
With every tear, a promise found,
In Elysian fields, love doth abound.

The garden breathes, in softest hues,
As dawn awakes with vibrant views.
For every loss, redemption comes,
In unity, our spirit drums.

A path bestowed, through trials gone,
Together strong, we carry on.
With hearts ignited, we seek the way,
In Elysian light, we greet the day.

With gentle hands, we heal the strain,
In fields of mercy, joy will reign.
For after the fall, we rise anew,
In love's embrace, our promise true.

Echoes of a Shattered Covenant

In whispered vows, the promise breaks,
A covenant torn, a world that aches.
Yet in the silence, echoes call,
To heal the bond that's bound to fall.

Through trembling hearts, we search for grace,
In fractured light, we find our place.
For broken paths can still lead home,
In unity, we cease to roam.

With every tear, a lesson learned,
In shadowed corners, hope's flame burned.
Together strong, we weave anew,
In echoes' dance, our spirits grew.

The threads of fate may twist and turn,
Yet in the fire, our souls will yearn.
For every promise that we break,
A chance for love, in truth we make.

In shattered faith, we seek the light,
To mend the bond, with endless might.
For echoes linger, through time they sing,
A fragile peace, in love we bring.

From Mourning to Sacred Light

In shadows deep where sorrows dwell,
We seek the truth, a whispered spell.
The heartache folds like morning mist,
Yet hope ignites with each sun-kissed.

From barren ground, a flower blooms,
It dances gently, dispelling glooms.
The spirit soars on wings of grace,
Finding solace in divine embrace.

Each tear that falls, a sacred stream,
Transforms our pain into a dream.
Awakening love from sorrow's night,
We walk together towards the light.

In humble prayer, our voices rise,
Through whispered winds and endless skies.
For in the loss, we learn to see,
The sacred bond of you and me.

From mourning's grasp, we take our flight,
Embracing life, a pure delight.
In every heart, a lantern bright,
Guides us from mourning to sacred light.

The Divine Stillness of Farewell

In silence deep, the heart does mourn,
Yet in this stillness, grace is born.
With every breath, a prayer anew,
Finding peace in what we knew.

The echoes fade, the day does part,
Still love remains within our heart.
In tender whispers, souls shall meet,
Where time's embrace can't taste defeat.

We gather strength from memories sweet,
In life's great dance, a bittersweet.
Through every trial, our spirits rise,
In joyful tears, we claim the skies.

The candle's glow, a beacon bright,
Guiding us safely through the night.
For in goodbye, we hold what's dear,
In divine stillness, there's no fear.

Though paths may change and seasons shift,
In every parting, we receive a gift.
The soul ascends, yet love will stay,
In the divine stillness of farewell's sway.

A Pilgrim's Journey Through Despair

Upon the road where shadows creep,
A pilgrim walks, through nights so deep.
With heavy heart, yet eyes aglow,
In despair's grip, the spirit grows.

Through valleys low, and mountains high,
Each step reveals a distant sky.
In loneliness, the strength we find,
Connecting with the heart and mind.

The scars we bear, the wounds that ache,
In trials deep, our souls awake.
As we traverse the paths of pain,
We find the light in every rain.

With every prayer, each question posed,
The journey weaves, the truth exposed.
In faith we stand, though lost we seem,
A pilgrim's path, a sacred dream.

For in despair, we seek the light,
And through the dark, we take our flight.
A journey shared, we rise and dare,
Embracing love, beyond despair.

Transfigured by Solitude

In solitude, the heart does sigh,
A quiet place where visions lie.
Through silent nights, our souls are free,
To dance within divinity.

The stillness speaks, a gentle call,
In shadows cast, we feel it all.
With every breath, we break the chain,
In solitude, we find the gain.

Through whispered thoughts, our spirits grow,
In sacred space, we come to know.
Transfigured by the love we seek,
The strength of one can make us weak.

Alone, yet not, we find the way,
In quietude, we learn to pray.
Embracing shadows, we ignite,
The flame of hope, as day takes flight.

Transfigured hearts in solitude,
Are woven tight in gratitude.
In every moment's tender grace,
We find our truth in love's embrace.

Redemption Through Ashes

From ashes we rise, a flicker of light,
In shadows of sorrow, we seek the bright.
With faith as our guide, we walk through the flame,
Embracing the trials, we find our true name.

In dust we discover the strength to endure,
Each heartbeat a promise, each prayer a cure.
Through darkness we wander, yet hope leads the way,
In the midst of our pain, new dawn breaks the day.

Through trials and tribulations, we learn to forgive,
In the depths of despair, we truly live.
Our spirits transformed, though battered and worn,
In the ashes we find the light to be reborn.

Hymns of the Brokenhearted

In the silence of grief, our voices unite,
Each tear that we shed, a testament bright.
With hymns on our lips, we mourn and we heal,
In the heartache we bear, the truth we reveal.

Echoes of sorrow, yet hope softly sings,
In valleys of shadow, redemption it brings.
We gather our scars as a badge of our fight,
In the depth of our darkness, we find the light.

Though broken and weary, together we stand,
With love as our anchor, clasping each hand.
In the symphony played by the shattered and torn,
We rise from the ashes, renewed and reborn.

The Sacred Return

In every lost path, a promise awaits,
A journey of souls, transcending the gates.
With whispers of grace, the spirit ignites,
Guiding us home, through the darkest of nights.

Each step we take, a ritual divine,
The sacred return, in love we entwine.
Forgiveness our banner, we lift high with pride,
In the warmth of connection, our hearts open wide.

Through mountains and valleys, our spirits will soar,
Each heartbeat a song, forever we explore.
In the echo of silence, the truth shall unfold,
The sacred return, a tale yet untold.

Grace in the Wake of Departed Souls

In the stillness of night, a whisper we feel,
The presence of loved ones, a bond that won't heal.
In their gentle embrace, we find our release,
With grace in our hearts, we discover sweet peace.

As seasons do change, so must we embrace,
The lessons of love in the empty space.
Through memories cherished, their light we hold dear,
In the wake of their passing, their whispers are clear.

Each tear that we shed, a river of grace,
With spirits beside us, we find our true place.
In every lost moment, love's echoes endure,
In the wake of departed, our hearts shall stay pure.

Revelations in the Ruins

In shadows deep, the whispers call,
Of ancient tales that still enthrall.
Through crumbled walls, a light does gleam,
Awakening hearts from a slumbered dream.

Dust of ages speaks in sighs,
Of once great prayers and hopeful cries.
Now silent stones bear witness true,
To every loss, each grace anew.

The ruins hold a sacred breath,
Where silent whispers conquer death.
Amidst decay, divinity shows,
In fractured lines, a purpose grows.

With every step through broken ground,
The pieces join, the lost are found.
In faith's embrace, we lift our eyes,
Revealing truths that never die.

So here we stand, amidst the past,
Finding beauty in shadows cast.
For even ruins, worn and bare,
Are hallowed ground, in spirit's care.

Fires of Faith After Loss

When sorrow strikes, the heart does ache,
Yet faith awakes, the spirit's wake.
In shadows dark, a flicker glows,
A sacred flame that softly grows.

Through trials fierce, the soul must trod,
Each tear a prayer, each sigh a nod.
For in the ashes of what was lost,
New life ignites, no matter the cost.

The ember's warmth calls forth the brave,
In quiet moments, the heart we save.
With every flame, our spirits rise,
A testament to love that never dies.

Through fires bright, we learn to see,
That loss can shape our destiny.
In every flicker, hope's rebirth,
A guiding light upon the earth.

So let us gather 'round this fire,
In shared embrace, hearts lift higher.
For in the flames, our truth we find,
A bond unbroken, our souls entwined.

Pilgrimage through Purgatory

Upon the path, the weary tread,
With burdens heavy, by hope we're led.
In shadows cast by burdens' weight,
A journey long, we navigate.

The road is rough, the sky is gray,
Yet every step ignites a way.
In silence found, redemption blooms,
As ancient sins release their glooms.

Each mile we walk reveals the past,
The choices made, the die that's cast.
Yet every heart, in longing speaks,
In search of peace, our spirit seeks.

In purgatory's grasp, we rise,
With every prayer, we touch the skies.
For every trial, we claim our grace,
And find our way through love's embrace.

So onward take this sacred quest,
For in the journey, we are blessed.
With every breath, we find our ground,
In pilgrimage, our truths are found.

The Veil of Forgotten Feasts

In hidden halls where shadows dwell,
The echoes of our stories swell.
Forgotten feasts, a memory's sigh,
As time wears thin, and candles die.

Each table set with love's fine thread,
In silence speaks of what is said.
The spirit's feast, though unseen, stays,
In heart's embrace through all our days.

Beneath the veil, the banquet waits,
Inviting souls through heaven's gates.
In every bite, a sacred grace,
A whisper sweet, of love's embrace.

As hymns of old begin to play,
The past and present weave their way.
With every laughter, tears may flow,
For in our loss, new joys may grow.

So let us lift our voice in praise,
For all the feasts of bygone days.
In remembering, our hearts convene,
In love's great feast, we are redeemed.

Shadows as Messengers

In the dusk where whispers grow,
Shadows stretch and softly flow.
They carry tales of grace and light,
Guiding souls through the night.

Each dark form has a voice to share,
Secrets held in twilight's care.
Step lightly where the spirits dwell,
For in their depths, the stories swell.

Lost in time, yet always near,
They cradle hopes, dissolve the fear.
With gentle rustles, they implore,
To seek the love that's at the core.

By moonlight's touch, we learn to see,
That shadows offer unity.
In their embrace, we find our way,
To brighter realms at break of day.

Parables of Love's Echo

In the garden where hearts bloom,
Echoes of love dispel the gloom.
Each petal tells a tale of grace,
Reflecting light upon each face.

The whispers ride on gentle breeze,
With every sigh, the spirit frees.
Through trials deep, love finds its song,
A melody that lasts lifelong.

In the stillness, we hear the call,
Binding us, both great and small.
Through hands reached out, and smiles exchanged,
A tapestry of lives arranged.

With every heartbeat, a sacred thread,
We weave our dreams where angels tread.
In echoes soft, the truth does dwell,
In love's embrace, we find our well.

The Canvas of the Healed Heart

On the canvas where colors blend,
A healed heart learns to transcend.
With strokes of kindness, joy defined,
Each hue reveals the love aligned.

Splashes bold against the dark,
Illuminate the smallest spark.
Brush away the stains of pain,
In beauty, let our hope remain.

When burdens weigh and shadows loom,
Artistry gives life to bloom.
In every curve, a story waits,
Transforming grief as the soul creates.

Faith in colors, rich and rare,
Draws forth the light from depths of care.
With every heartbeat, a new design,
In the tapestry of love, we find.

Divine Healing in the Night

Beneath the stars, where silence breathes,
Divine whispers float like leaves.
In shadows deep, the spirits wane,
Yet healing flows through every pain.

As moonlit beams caress the ground,
In sacred spaces, peace is found.
A gentle balm for weary soul,
Restoring faith, making whole.

With every prayer that breaks the dark,
Light ignites a hopeful spark.
In stillness wrapped, we find our way,
To trust the dawn that follows day.

In night's embrace, our hearts align,
With love that flows, a true design.
So in the quiet, know you're blessed,
Divine healing gives us rest.

Ascension in Heart's Ashes

From the depths of sorrow, we rise,
Through the flames of loss, our spirit flies.
In the ashes of heart, we find our birth,
A dance of resurrection, a sacred mirth.

With each tear that falls, a seed is sown,
In the garden of grace, we're not alone.
We gather the fragments, the broken shards,
Whispers of hope, our prayers as guards.

The phoenix within, it learns to soar,
In the light of the dawn, we seek out more.
Holding our wounds as a testament,
In the struggle and pain, love is lent.

Every moment of silence sings the hymn,
Of those who have risen, their light not dim.
In the embrace of sorrow, we find our way,
To the morning of joy, where shadows play.

So let us ascend, in faith we'll trust,
In the ashes of heart, there's life and dust.
For every ending, a glorious start,
In the tapestry woven, ascends the heart.

The Alchemy of Grief

In the crucible of tears, we transform,
The heart knows no silence, nor calm before storm.
Alchemy of sorrow, a sacred rite,
From leaden despair, we gather the light.

Each sorrowful echo, a lesson learned,
In the fires of grief, our spirits are burned.
We turn the dark matter to gold so bright,
Emerging as souls, with wings taking flight.

In the chambers of loss, wisdom unfurls,
We traverse the shadows, as memory swirls.
Casting aside burdens, we dance through the night,
The alchemy of grief reveals pure insight.

With every lament, a melody flows,
A tapestry woven in loss, it still grows.
For within every tear, a treasure unseen,
In the heart's ancient book, love reigns supreme.

So let us embrace, what sorrow can teach,
For in the abyss, no limit it screeches.
Through grief's gentle hands, we're shaped to believe,
In the alchemy of life, we learn to receive.

Embered Souls, Reclaimed

From embers we rise, with spirit afire,
Reclaimed from the ashes, our hearts aspire.
In the glow of redemption, we find our home,
With every lost dream, a place to roam.

Each flicker of hope, a beacon so bright,
Illuminates paths in the stillness of night.
Together we gather, the embered souls,
Binding our journeys, as the universe rolls.

In the forge of despair, we're tempered anew,
With strength from our struggles, we break through.
Not shackled by chains, but soaring high,
In the cradle of faith, where shadows fly.

The whispers of past, like echoes entwined,
In the tapestry woven, love's thread we find.
Through the fire of trials, our essence is formed,
Ember to spirit, our hearts now warmed.

So here we ignite, with purpose our aim,
In the embered souls, we rekindle the flame.
A testament written in grace and in trust,
Through the trials of life, rise we must.

The Hymn of Broken Altar

In the broken altar, we gather our fears,
With hearts laid open, we shed silent tears.
Each fragment a prayer, a testament true,
To the love that survives, in all that we do.

The stones may be chipped, but the spirit remains,
A sacred connection, through losses and gains.
These hymns of the heart, though twisted and torn,
Resound even louder, in the midst of the scorn.

So let us not falter, nor cower in pride,
In the cracks of our faith, new strength will abide.
With hands raised in worship, we sing through the pain,
For the hymn of our hearts, like softest refrain.

Each note tells a story of grace that will flow,
From the depths of our sorrow, in love we will grow.
The broken altar sings of what we have learned,\nIn the
journey of faith, our hopes are returned.

So we rise from the ruins, reclaiming our vows,
With the hymn of the broken, we honor our brows.
United in spirit, our voices are clear,
For in every fracture, love conquers fear.

From Grief to Grace

In shadows deep where sorrows dwell,
Hope flickers low, a distant bell.
Yet through the night, a whisper calls,
Transforming grief as daylight falls.

With every tear that falls like rain,
A seed of faith grows strong from pain.
Embracing loss, we find our way,
In silent prayers, the heart will stay.

A journey carved through trials faced,
Leads to the arms of loving grace.
In moments dark, we learn to see,
The path of light, our destiny.

From ashes rise reborn anew,
The warmth of love, a radiant hue.
For in the depths of our despair,
The hands of time will guide us there.

Embrace the dawn, let sorrow cease,
In every wound, find sweet release.
From grief, we craft our sacred space,
And bloom again with boundless grace.

The Divine Parable of Regeneration

In ancient tales where truth unfolds,
A parable of love retold.
From dust to life, the Spirit breathes,
In every soul, a purpose weaves.

The prodigal who seeks to roam,
Returns at last, the heart finds home.
For as the sun sets, hope remains,
In every heart, redemption gains.

The shepherd calls, the lost are found,
In gentle grace, their hearts unbound.
The willow bends but does not break,
In every trial, new paths we make.

The lilies bloom in fields of strife,
Reflecting love and sacred life.
From barren ground, a garden grows,
With every tear, His mercy flows.

In waves of change, we find our song,
Through struggle, we make our spirits strong.
In each regeneration's flight,
The dance of hope ignites the night.

Souls Awakened from Silence

In silence deep, a spark ignites,
Awakens souls to heavenly sights.
From slumber's grip, they start to rise,
With voices lifted to the skies.

A whisper soft, the Spirit's call,
Breaks through the chains that bind us all.
In every heart, a song awaits,
The light of love, our souls create.

In unity, we find our strength,
Together journey, go the length.
A chorus formed from every chest,
In harmony, our souls find rest.

As dawn unfolds its golden hue,
The world awakens, fresh and new.
From silence springs a sacred roar,
As hearts unite forevermore.

For every soul that dares to dream,
A sacred river flows like a stream.
In silent depths, the truth does shine,
Awakened hearts, forever divine.

The Garden of Withered Blossoms

In autumn's breath, the petals fall,
A garden whispers, echoes call.
Withered blooms, a tale of grace,
In every petal, life's embrace.

Once vibrant hues now muted gray,
Yet beauty lingers in decay.
For in the dying, life renews,
The cycle spins, the heart imbues.

Amongst the thorns, there lies a dream,
Of brighter days and gentle stream.
Through sorrow's grasp, we find our peace,
A bittersweet that will not cease.

In shadowed paths where memories weep,
The garden rests, its promises keep.
For every end, a new beginning,
In silence found, the heart's soft singing.

So let the blossoms fade and fall,
For life persists through nature's call.
In withered grace, we learn to see,
The beauty held in mystery.

The Book of Shattered Mends

In pages torn and worn with time,
The whispers of the lost align.
Each tear a tale, each crack a breath,
And hope reborn beyond all death.

With hands that heal and hearts that bind,
We gather shards that fate resigned.
In sacred light, we stitch the seams,
And turn our sorrows into dreams.

The ink of tears, a sacred flow,
Penning our trials as we grow.
With faith, we write, though shadows loom,
Our spirits rise from deepest gloom.

As saints in search of solace find,
The strength of love in every kind.
We learn to mend what once was whole,
And carve the path to heal the soul.

Thus, in the book of shattered mends,
We find the grace that never ends.
Through every scar, a lesson taught,
In every loss, a victory sought.

Ascending from Tombs of Heartache

From shadows deep where sorrows dwell,
We rise as phoenixes from hell.
With wings of faith and hearts ablaze,
We seek the light in darkest days.

Each tomb a marker of the past,
Yet in our hearts, we find at last
The strength to climb, to reach, to soar,
As angels guide us evermore.

The echoes of the pain we bear,
Transform to hymns of hope and prayer.
With every step, we shed the weight,
And in forgiveness, we create.

Through valleys low and mountains high,
We raise our voices to the sky.
The burdens fade, our spirits sing,
In unity, we find our wings.

Ascending from tombs of heartache,
We forge a path that none can take.
In grace we walk, in love we stand,
Together, hand in hand, we land.

The Embrace of the Transcended

In realms where souls entwine and bend,
We find the arms of the transcended.
Their light envelops every fear,
A warmth that draws the willing near.

With every touch, we shed the past,
Embraced by love, our shadows cast.
In unity, our spirits soar,
Connected to the Evermore.

As whispers soft as evening prayer,
Awaken us to love's sweet care.
We dance in sacred, timeless grace,
Each heartbeat echoes, 'You are safe.'

The veil between just fades away,
In presence, we are led to play.
Our fears dissolve, our doubts take flight,
In truth's embrace, we find the light.

Thus, in the arms of love we dwell,
A promise held, a sacred spell.
The embrace of the transcended calls,
And in that love, we rise, we fall.

Resounding in the Silence

In quiet moments, whispers rise,
A symphony beneath the skies.
Through stillness, truths unfold their grace,
In silent realms, we find our place.

The heartbeats drum a gentle song,
Resounding where we all belong.
With every pause, a prayer is formed,
In silence deep, our souls are warmed.

In absence loud, the spirit speaks,
A balm for those who seek the peaks.
The echoes of the calm provide,
A refuge where the heart can hide.

Within this quiet, visions bloom,
And love illuminates the gloom.
The voice of God, a soft caress,
In every silence, we are blessed.

So let us dwell in peace profound,
In every heartbeat, love is found.
Resounding in the silence, we
Awake to all we're meant to be.

The Prayer of the Unloved

In shadows deep, I call Your name,
A whisper lost, yet still aflame.
Embrace me, Lord, in my despair,
For in this void, I seek Your care.

With aching heart, my spirit bends,
I long for love that never ends.
Each tear I shed, a humble plea,
To find in pain, Your grace in me.

O Shepherd kind, I seek Your face,
In every wound, let mercy trace.
Illuminate my path anew,
With gentle hands, I turn to You.

The world may turn its gaze away,
Yet still, in faith, I choose to stay.
For in this dark, Your light doth shine,
My heart is held; I am divine.

So lift me up, O King of Kings,
With every breath, my spirit sings.
In love's embrace, I find my way,
The unloved child, by night and day.

Messages from the Depths

From depths unknown, I hear Your voice,
In silence, Lord, You guide my choice.
Each echo whispers hope anew,
In shadowed valleys, I seek You.

The shadows stretch, but faith won't break,
In storms of doubt, my heart won't shake.
You speak in waves, in gentle sighs,
Your presence felt, as darkness flies.

With every trial, a lesson learned,
In fiery paths, my spirit burned.
Yet from the ashes, I arise,
Reminded still, love never dies.

Your message flows like rivers wide,
In troubled waters, You abide.
I cling to truths, both pure and strong,
In depths of night, I sing my song.

So let me hear, Your sacred word,
In every note, my soul is stirred.
With faith as anchor, I stand tall,
In depthless love, I give my all.

Ascension after the Abyss

Beneath the weight of darkened skies,
I lost my way, but chose to rise.
With every step, the shadows flee,
In strength renewed, I'm born to be.

When depths of sorrow held my soul,
You lifted me, You made me whole.
Through trials fierce, I sought Your grace,
The path of light, my soul's embrace.

From darkest nights, the dawn appeared,
In faith's embrace, I cast my fears.
Your hands, O Lord, they guide my flight,
In every fall, You are my light.

I climbed the mountains, faced the storms,
In Your great love, my spirit warms.
With every breath, I claim the way,
From abyss deep, to brighter day.

So let the heavens sing my praise,
In joy I walk, in love I gaze.
Ascend with me, O skies above,
Forever bound in endless love.

The Mountaintop of Restoration

Upon the mountaintop so high,
I lift my heart, I touch the sky.
In quiet moments, peace descends,
Restoration comes, as grace transcends.

With every breath, I feel You near,
Your presence calms my every fear.
In splendor bright, Your love displayed,
Restoring hope where darkness played.

I see the valleys, far below,
The trials faced, the seeds we sow.
From pain to purpose, life reborn,
In every dawn, Your light is sworn.

O mountain high, my refuge strong,
In valleys low, I still belong.
Your faithfulness my guiding star,
In every wound, love's healing scar.

So lift me up, O Lord of grace,
In every step, I seek Your face.
The mountaintop, where spirits soar,
In restoration, forevermore.

Threads Woven in Grief

In shadows deep, where silence grows,
The heart weeps soft, a river flows.
Each tear a thread, a bond divine,
In mourning's cloak, our souls entwine.

With whispered prayers, we seek the light,
To guide the lost, to mend the night.
Through every ache, a lesson learned,
In grief, the fire of love is burned.

The fabric coarse, yet woven strong,
In sorrow's arms, we find our song.
In every thread, a hope reframed,
With every loss, the heart is named.

And when we've stitched our wounds with care,
We rise anew, our spirits bare.
For in the grief, we've come to see,
The beauty born from agony.

So hold each thread, let memories stay,
In every fold, a brighter day.
In sorrow's weave, our paths adjourn,
In love's embrace, our souls return.

Ceremonies of Transformation

In sacred space, where spirits meet,
We gather close, our hearts in beat.
With hands raised high, we dance and sing,
In celebration, our souls take wing.

The fires burn, a cleansing flame,
Invoking change, we speak your name.
Through rituals rich, we shed our past,
In every heartbeat, a truth holds fast.

Emerging from the ashes grey,
We cast away the old, the fray.
With every breath, new purpose found,
In transformation, love's voice resounds.

In circles formed, we chant our vows,
To honor life, to cherish now.
Each moment framed, a treasure sought,
In holy acts, our spirits caught.

So may we rise, a phoenix bright,
Embracing change, embracing light.
In ceremonies, our souls ignite,
To follow truth and seek the right.

Resounding in the Aftermath

When silence falls, and echoes fade,
The heart must learn, the soul be laid.
In whispers soft, the truth takes flight,
Resounding still through darkest night.

In aftermath, we gather strength,
To tread the storms, to go the length.
With every trial, our spirits rise,
In fierce resolve, we claim the skies.

Though shadows loom, hope shines anew,
In every breath, a promise true.
Through shattered dreams, we find the way,
In resilience, we choose to stay.

With open hearts, we share our tale,
In bonds of faith, we shall prevail.
Each wound a mark, a badge of grace,
In unity, we find our place.

So let us stand, the brave, the kind,
In aftermath, our love defined.
Resound our voices, ever clear,
In strength and hope, we persevere.

The Light in the Wilderness

In wilderness, where shadows creep,
A glimmer shines, the promise deep.
Through tangled paths, the way unknown,
The light within, we call our own.

In solitude, we seek the flame,
With every step, we speak your name.
Through trials faced, through doubts we bear,
In faith's embrace, we find the air.

The stars above, our guides at night,
In darkest hour, we sense the light.
With every breath, the spirit sighs,
To lead us forth, to help us rise.

So let us walk, though lost we seem,
With hearts aligned, we'll chase the dream.
In wilderness, we dance with fear,
Yet in the light, we hold you near.

For every storm, we weather bold,
In sacred stories, our truths unfold.
In wilderness, we find our song,
The light within, we all belong.

A New Testament of the Soul

From ashes we rise, in faith we abide,
With whispers of grace, the spirit's guide.
Each tear that we shed, a promise to keep,
In the light of His love, our hearts will leap.

In darkness we wander, yet hope shines bright,
A beacon of mercy, our path ignites.
Through trials we stumble, together we stand,
With hands intertwined, we follow His plan.

The mountains may tremble, the rivers may roar,
Yet the courage within us opens the door.
For every lost soul, a prayer takes flight,
In the embrace of His peace, we find our light.

The journey is long, yet tender the way,
With faith as our armor, we rise every day.
The whispers of angels, a heavenly sound,
In the depths of our hearts, His love knows no bound.

And when time shall cease, and all has been told,
In the triumph of spirit, we shall be bold.
For a testament written, in love we behold,
The essence of truth that eternally unfolds.

The Last Supper of Sorrow

In shadows we gather, on this fateful night,
With bread broken softly, hearts filled with light.
The cup that is raised, a moment of grace,
In remembrance we pause, in the sacred space.

Each whisper a prayer, each glance a farewell,
The bond of the faithful, we wear like a spell.
In sorrow we feast, for joy is divine,
In the depths of our sorrow, our souls intertwine.

The table is set, but the silence is loud,
For the burden we carry, we feel so proud.
In the bitterness shared, we find our release,
In the sorrowful cup, there lies holy peace.

With every last crumb, the memories fade,
Yet the love in our hearts is deeply portrayed.
For in every shadow, a light will be found,
In the last supper shared, our spirits unbound.

So we raise our voices, as one we shall sing,
In a chorus of hope, a new offering.
With the taste of our tears, we honor the night,
For in sorrow's embrace, we find our true light.

Divine Engagement with the Past

In the garden of shadows, history waits,
The echoes of ages, the unlocking of gates.
With each step we take, we honor the plight,
For the lessons of yore guide us to light.

The pages we turn are written in tears,
In the depths of our heart, we face ancient fears.
For the wisdom of old calls out from the grave,
In the embrace of the past, we learn to be brave.

Each moment we gather, a tapestry spun,
Woven with threads of the many and one.
In the whispers of time, we find our way back,
To the roots of our spirit, the beautiful track.

With faith as our lantern, we wander and seek,
For the truth of our being is tender yet meek.
The stories of trials, joy, and despair,
In divine engagement, our souls bared bare.

So let us not falter, but dance in the rain,
For the past is a canvas painted with pain.
Yet love is the brush that colors our heart,
In the divine engagement, we shall not depart.

The Archive of Aftermath

In the silence that follows, a whisper is found,
An archive of aftermath, sacred and sound.
Each sorrowful tale, a chapter of grace,
In the echo of losses, we seek His embrace.

With pages turned slowly, the lessons unfold,
In the warmth of remembrance, our spirits are told.
For every heart shattered, a rebuild begins,
In the dance of the ashes, our journey spins.

The scars that we bear are stories of light,
In the depths of the night, they shine ever bright.
For the aftermath speaks, with a voice so true,
In the hope that arises, we start life anew.

In the archive of echoes, compassion's the key,
To unlock the doors of our souls, we must see.
With faith as our compass, we tread on this path,
In the aftermath woven, we harvest the wrath.

So let us remember, as we gather here,
In the archive of aftermath, love conquers fear.
For every misstep is a dance with the divine,
And in our shared journey, our hearts intertwine.

Covenant of the Wounded

In shadows deep, the cry ascends,
A covenant made where sorrow bends.
Hearts broken, yet hope ignites,
In love's embrace, the spirit fights.

Wounds that bleed, but heal to grace,
A sacred trust in this holy place.
Through trials faced, we rise anew,
In every tear, His mercy grew.

The promise sings in whispered prayer,
Each soul redeemed, each heart laid bare.
With hands outstretched, in faith we stand,
Together bound, in sacred land.

In darkest nights, the stars align,
A guiding light, His plan divine.
Through every storm, we find our way,
The wounded hearts shall learn to pray.

So let us walk this path of love,
With strength bestowed from high above.
In brokenness, our spirits soar,
In the covenant, we trust once more.

Songs of the Surviving

In the quiet dawn, the songs arise,
Voices lifted to the skies.
From ashes born, the spirit sings,
In every heart, redemption brings.

Through trials harsh, through darkest days,
We search for light in hidden ways.
With courage fierce, we claim our tale,
Through pain endured, we shall not pale.

The melodies of hope resound,
In faith, our strength is truly found.
Each note a prayer, each chord a dream,
In unity, we stand, we beam.

With every step, we learn to dance,
Embracing life, we take our chance.
Though storms may rage and shadows fall,
Together brave, we heed the call.

So sing aloud, O hearts that heal,
In joy, in pain, let truth reveal.
The songs of those who rise and fight,
Shall echo strong, in endless light.

Divine Interludes of Solace

In sacred moments, we find our peace,
Divine interludes where worries cease.
In whispered prayers, the heart takes flight,
In stillness found, we sense the light.

Each breath a blessing, each sigh a hymn,
In quiet spaces, our souls can swim.
Through trials faced, through burdens bore,
We seek the solace, forevermore.

Among the stars, His hand we trace,
A gentle touch, a warm embrace.
In every pause, the mystery glows,
In divine silence, our spirit knows.

From chaos veiled, we draw the calm,
In every storm, we find the balm.
With open hearts, we come undone,
In solace sweet, we're one with One.

So let us linger in these hours,
In divine presence, love empowers.
Through interludes, our spirits sing,
In softest whispers, joy takes wing.

Elysian Dreams of Renewal

In twilight's glow, our dreams unfold,
Elysian visions, bright and bold.
With every dawn, the spirit wakes,
In gentle light, each heart remakes.

Through valleys deep and mountains high,
We seek the truth, we soar the sky.
In every struggle, we find the grace,
Eternal love that time can't erase.

The colors burst in morning's kiss,
In vibrant hues, we find our bliss.
Awakened souls in rapture dance,
In every moment, love's sweet chance.

With hands held tight, we forge the path,
In unity, we feel the wrath.
In dreams of peace, our hearts align,
The world transformed, as souls entwine.

So let us dream, O spirits bright,
In every shadow, seek the light.
For in renewal, we find our place,
In Elysian realms, we seek His face.

Signs of Resurrection in Midst of Loss

In shadows deep, where sorrows dwell,
A whisper stirs, as hope can tell.
From ashes rise, the spirit's glow,
In darkest night, the love will flow.

Though tears may fall, the heart does mend,
In every crack, there's light to send.
The soul's rebirth in every sigh,
With faith anew, the dreams will fly.

Through bitter storms, we journey forth,
In sacred grace, we find our worth.
The sacred dawn, a promise made,
In loss, our hearts, forever stayed.

Each wound a sign of life once lived,
In brokenness, the gift we give.
For every end, a start is near,
In unity, we conquer fear.

Forever etched in memory,
In love's embrace, we shall be free.
The signs of life dance in the night,
Resurrection's breath, our guiding light.

Apotheosis of the Heart's Remains

In silence deep, where echoes fade,
A heart once bold, in shadows laid.
From sorrow's depth, the soul ascends,
In whispered prayers, a love transcends.

Each fragment lost, the spirit's art,
In every piece, a sacred heart.
With tender grace, we weave the strands,
To craft anew with gentle hands.

The ashes warm, ignite the flame,
In quiet strength, love calls our name.
Through trials faced, the truth we find,
In every tear, the ties that bind.

From dusk to dawn, the journey we take,
In every choice, the steps we make.
The heart's remains, a sacred song,
In harmony, we still belong.

In moments small, the beauty grows,
In hearts united, love still flows.
Apotheosis, where we stand,
Beyond the veil, hand in hand.

Covenant of the Solitary Flame

In night's embrace, where shadows fall,
A flame aglow, a guiding call.
In solitude, the spirit yearns,
For solace found as the heart learns.

This covenant, a bond unseen,
In quiet nights, where hopes have been.
The flickering light, a promise made,
Within the stillness, love won't fade.

In moments brief, the light expands,
A universal touch, like golden strands.
With fervor strong, the heart ignites,
In solitude, we seek the heights.

Together yet, we walk alone,
In every heart, the seeds are sown.
A solitary flame, the truth reveals,
In shadows deep, the spirit heals.

With every breath, this pact we share,
Through trials faced, a sacred care.
In unity, our depths proclaim,
The covenant of the solitary flame.

Spirit's Song Beyond the Grave

In twilight's glow, the spirit sings,
Of love that soars on gentle wings.
Beyond the grave, the echoes flow,
A timeless tune, forever glow.

Through veils of time, the heart can hear,
The songs of those who linger near.
In every breeze, a soft embrace,
The spirit's dance, a sacred space.

With every note, the memories fade,
Yet in the light, our peace is made.
In whispered winds, the truth reveals,
A bond unbroken, that truly heals.

In joy and pain, the song we share,
In every heart, a love laid bare.
The spirit's hymn, a melody bright,
Guiding us home through darkest night.

Though bodies rest, the souls will soar,
To realms of grace, forevermore.
In love's embrace, we come alive,
In spirit's song, together thrive.

Birth from the Buried

In shadows deep, the seed does lie,
A whisper of hope beneath the sky.
From soil rich, and darkness frayed,
New life emerges, unafraid.

With gentle rains, the Spirit weeps,
Nurturing dreams that softly creep.
In every heart, a spark ignites,
Guided by the starry nights.

From ashes past, we rise anew,
A sacred dance, a covenant true.
Embrace the dawn, let sorrows cease,
For in our pain, we find release.

Heaven's choir sings in tune,
Echoed in the silver moon.
Each breath a prayer, a call to grace,
In every moment, He finds His place.

As life unfolds in sacred text,
The buried dreams, forever vexed.
Yet from the dark, we light the flame,
In unity, we bless His name.

The Mosaic of Memories

In each small shard, the stories weave,
Moments cherished, never leave.
Fragments of laughter, tears that fall,
A timeless tapestry, binding all.

Each memory holds a sacred spark,
Whispers soft, guiding in the dark.
Pieces of faith, love's gentle art,
Together they play the pulse of the heart.

Through trials faced, we find the thread,
A path of grace where angels tread.
Every sorrow turns to light,
Mosaics formed in darkest night.

In gathering clouds, the promise gleams,
Reflections deep, we chase our dreams.
The echoes linger, forever true,
A living portrait, me and you.

So let us treasure each fleeting part,
In this grand design, we share a heart.
For in the mosaic, our souls entwine,
Bearing witness to the divine.

Epic of the Enduring

Through valleys low and mountains high,
The Spirit moves, our hearts reply.
In every struggle, we find our song,
An epic tale where we belong.

With every tear, a river flows,
Washing doubts, as faith glows.
In shadows cast, we learn to rise,
Strengthened by love, we touch the skies.

The battle rages, yet hope stands tall,
In unity's grasp, we will not fall.
With hands uplifted, we face the storm,
In the heat of trials, our spirits warm.

Through darkest nights, the dawn does break,
Revealing paths that love will make.
An epic forged in fire's might,
With every heartbeat, we seek the light.

Together we journey, hand in hand,
Across the seas, we take a stand.
In the epic's end, forever one,
A testament of love thus spun.

Revelations in the Wound

In every wound, a lesson sleeps,
A silent voice that gently weeps.
From pain we rise, our spirits grow,
Through cracks of sorrow, love will flow.

In scars we bear, the truth is laid,
A map of battles fiercely played.
Each one tells tales of grace and might,
In darkness found, we seek the light.

Revelations bloom from aching hearts,
In wounds we find where healing starts.
What shatters us, makes us whole,
In every tear, we grasp our soul.

From grief's embrace, we rise again,
A resurrection from the pain.
With open arms, we hold the past,
In every moment, the die is cast.

So cherish wounds, for they reveal,
The sacred truth in every heal.
With love, we turn each scar to grace,
In revelations, we find our place.

Rebirth Beneath the Ruins

Amidst the stones where shadows dwell,
Hope flickers soft as a distant bell.
From ashes rise the dreams once lost,
In faith we find our worth, our cost.

New life emerges from despair's hold,
In sacred soil, our spirits bold.
With every breath, the past is shed,
A garden blooms where once was dread.

The light of dawn breaks through the night,
Illuminating the path of right.
Each tear that falls, a promise made,
In sorrow's grip, new joys invade.

With hands uplifted, we seek the grace,
In the ruins, love finds its place.
The heart reborn, a sacred fire,
From the depths of loss, we rise, aspire.

Together we walk, side by side,
In this journey, let hope be our guide.
Beneath the ruins, our souls take flight,
In the embrace of love, we find the light.

Transcendent Shadows

In twilight's glow where whispers roam,
The shadows dance, but do not own.
In silence, sacred truth is found,
Transcendent whispers, a heavenly sound.

Each shadow holds a story deep,
Of love and loss, of souls that weep.
Yet through the dark, the light breaks free,
A guiding star for you and me.

When burdens bear upon the heart,
And hope seems lost, we play our part.
A flicker bright amidst the night,
With faith, we claim our sacred right.

Through trials faced, our spirits soar,
In shadows' depths, we find much more.
A tapestry of grace unfolds,
In every thread, the truth beholds.

So walk with me in shadows cast,
Together, let our fears be past.
Transcend the doubt, embrace the whole,
In the shadow's depth, we find our soul.

A Pilgrim's Heart

With every step, the journey calls,
In pilgrimage, the spirit sprawls.
Through valleys low and mountains high,
We seek the path where angels fly.

The pilgrim's heart, both pure and brave,
Navigates the waters, the stormy wave.
In every trial, a lesson clear,
In faith, we conquer every fear.

With open hands, we share the road,
Bearing each other's heavy load.
In kindness given, grace returns,
A fire of love within us burns.

As footsteps blend with ages past,
The echo of the saints hold fast.
A tapestry of stories spun,
In every thread, our lives are one.

So journey forth, oh heart so true,
In every dawn, His light shines through.
A pilgrim's heart, forever free,
In sacred love, our spirits see.

Echoes of the Unreturned

In quiet halls where echoes dwell,
The whispers carry stories well.
Of souls departed, journeys vast,
In every sigh, their shadows cast.

Yet still we feel their presence here,
In every laugh and every tear.
The unreturned, they gently guide,
In love's embrace, they still abide.

Through memories etched upon the heart,
They live within, they never part.
In sacred bonds that time can't fray,
Their light remains to guide our way.

So let us honor what they gave,
In quiet moments, we are brave.
For in our hearts, they find a home,
In every path they help us roam.

As echoes linger through the night,
We find our peace in love's true light.
The unreturned, forever near,
In every breath, they reappear.

Oracle of the Withering Heart

In shadows deep, the whispers call,
An oracle waits, a fate for all.
Withering hearts in silence weep,
Their secrets buried, buried deep.

Hear the echoes of love's refrain,
In the solitude, we feel the pain.
Yet through the tears, a light may gleam,
Hope shines bright, a fragile dream.

The weary travel, lost in night,
Searching for meaning, craving the light.
Yet the oracle speaks softly still,
Embrace the path, bend to His will.

In sacred truth, the heart can mend,
With every wound, there's chance to tend.
For every withering, a blooming chance,
In faith's embrace, souls will dance.

The Pathway Through Sorrow's Vale

Through sorrow's vale, the pathway lies,
Beneath the pain, the spirit cries.
Each step we take, a heavy cost,
Yet in our loss, we find what's lost.

The guiding stars through tears appear,
Their gentle glow, a balm to fear.
In every shadow, grace will gleam,
A flicker of faith—a sacred dream.

Remember not the dark alone,
For in the grief, love's seeds are sown.
With every heartbeat, a rhythm stirs,
Together we rise, as hope occurs.

Through valleys deep, we walk in trust,
For from despair, our hearts adjust.
Each sorrow fades, as light will grow,
On pathways forged by love's pure flow.

Faith's Gentle Hand in Loss

In loss we find, a gentle hand,
That leads us forth, to promise land.
Though shadows gather, dark as night,
In faith's embrace, we find our light.

The wounds will heal, though scars remain,
A testament to love's sweet pain.
In every sigh, a prayer ascends,
For in the heart, true faith transcends.

As we journey through each tear,
We feel the presence drawing near.
In whispered hopes, our souls align,
With every loss, divinity's sign.

So hand in hand, we walk the road,
With faith as guide, our heavy load.
In the stillness, we shall find,
The gentle hand that binds mankind.

Cathedral of Lost Affections

In the cathedral, hearts resound,
Lost affections, sacred ground.
The pews adorned with whispered dreams,
Echoes linger, or so it seems.

The stained glass filters light so pure,
Each hue reveals a love demure.
Through memories, the spirit wails,
Within these walls, the heart unveils.

But love is not just grief we bear,
It breathes the air, a silent prayer.
In every corner, joy has bled,
From all that's lost, love's light is spread.

So gather here, in solace sweet,
Where shadows fade and spirits meet.
In this cathedral, though we grieve,
In lost affections, we believe.

Testament of the Wounded Heart

In shadows deep, where sorrows dwell,
A heart once whole, now speaks its shell.
Through trials faced, a voice refined,
In whispered prayers, salvation find.

With every tear, a lesson learned,
In pain, the soul so brightly burned.
Each scar a tale, a journey's mark,
To light the path within the dark.

The echoes of the past shall guide,
Through valleys low, where fears reside.
With faith as armor, hope as shield,
The wounded heart shall never yield.

A testament of love profound,
In every heartbeat, grace is found.
For even broken, beauty stays,
In the embrace of higher ways.

So let it rise, this heart once sore,
To dance again on faith's own floor.
In every wound, a seed shall grow,
The testament, for all to know.

The Divine Artistry of Healing

In silence deep, the Spirit weaves,
The threads of hope through hearts that grieve.
A gentle touch, a soothing balm,
In every breath, a sacred calm.

Through shattered dreams, new visions rise,
In every tear, a chance to prize.
The artistry of hands divine,
In every wound, a destined sign.

The tapestry of grace unfolds,
In colors bright, the heart beholds.
Each knot and twist, a story shared,
In faith's embrace, we are prepared.

With every pulse, the healing flows,
A river strong, where mercy grows.
To mend the soul, to claim the light,
In darkest times, love shines so bright.

Thus, let us walk on paths anew,
With hearts healed strong, in wisdom true.
For in His hands, we rise and stand,
The divine artistry at hand.

Wings of a Dying Flame

Upon the dusk, the whispers blend,
Of memories lost and dreams that bend.
The flame once bright begins to fade,
Yet in its heart, love's light is laid.

Though winds may howl, and shadows creep,
In quiet strength, the spirit keeps.
With wings outstretched, though scorched and worn,
From ashes rise, a soul reborn.

Each flicker holds a tale untold,
In embers warm, true hearts unfold.
The beauty found in trials faced,
In dying flame, grace is traced.

Through darkest nights, the stars emerge,
In sacred space, the spirits surge.
With fervent hope, we search and seek,
Though flames may dim, the heart is meek.

So let us soar on dreams undone,
With wings that dance beneath the sun.
In every end, a brand new start,
The wings of love embrace the heart.

The Altar of Abandonment

In quietude, the heart surrenders,
To all that's lost, where love remembers.
Upon the altar, burdens laid,
The soul finds peace in silence made.

Each whispered prayer, a gentle guide,
In yielding heart, the truth confides.
To leave behind the weight we bear,
A promise held in tender care.

With open hands, we seek to part,
From fears that clutch the weary heart.
In vulnerability, strength is found,
In letting go, we become unbound.

The altar stands, a sacred space,
Where grace abounds, and love embraces.
In casting fears upon the flame,
We rise anew, in joy we claim.

Thus, let us bow, in humble trust,
To dance with faith, in love we must.
In every end, a chance to grow,
The altar of abandonment shall glow.

The Quiet Blessing of Letting Go

In silence, shadows gently part,
The burdens lift from weary heart.
A whisper calls from deep within,
To find the peace where love has been.

Like autumn leaves that grace the ground,
In letting go, new life is found.
A fragile trust in time's embrace,
Awakens joy, unveils His grace.

The river flows, it knows the way,
Through valleys dark, to light of day.
Like faithful hands, it shapes the stone,
Reminding all, we're not alone.

With every tear that falls like rain,
A lesson learned, a heart unchained.
In yielding softly to the flow,
We find the strength in letting go.

Embrace the dawn that breaks anew,
For every ending sparks a view.
The quiet blessing, pure and clear,
In every loss, His love draws near.

Ascended from Night's Embrace

Beneath the stars, a soul takes flight,
From shadows deep, into the light.
The heav'nly chorus starts to sing,
As hope emerges on golden wing.

Each tear that falls, a sacred rite,
Transforms the dark to brilliant light.
In stillness found, the heart takes pause,
In whispers soft, His will, our cause.

The path we walk, though fraught with fear,
Is guided by a love so dear.
The night may hold its fierce embrace,
But morning breaks with boundless grace.

The spirits rise on winds of prayer,
Our burdens lifted, light as air.
From darkness sprung, in faith we soar,
Ascended high, we are reborn.

So let the dawn embrace your soul,
In faith, we find the sacred whole.
For every night that's cast in shade,
A promise made, our fears allayed.

The Sacred Garden of Forgotten Love

In whispered winds, the memories sway,
A garden grown, where heart once lay.
Each petal soft, a tale untold,
In colors bright, a love unfolds.

The quiet blooms of yesteryears,
In flowers bloom, we tend our tears.
A sacred space, where laughter rings,
In echo's dance, the heart still sings.

Forgotten paths, yet still they gleam,
Like starlit skies that awaken dreams.
For every rose with thorns it bears,
Reflects the love that lingers there.

In sunlight's touch, the shadows fade,
Yet roots remain in love's cascade.
With every breath, this garden grows,
Embracing all, while softly flows.

Though seasons change and time departs,
The sacred garden tends our hearts.
For love once known will ever be,
A testament to memory.

Eulogy for a Fading Star

In twilight's glow, a star descends,
A tale of love, as daylight ends.
With gentle grace, it leaves the sky,
A luminous tear that bids goodbye.

We gather here, in reverence sing,
Of fleeting light and heart's own wing.
The echo lingers, soft yet clear,
A legacy that draws us near.

Each sparkle bright, a moment caught,
In fathoms deep, where dreams are sought.
Though stars may fade, their glow remains,
In every beat, their essence reigns.

Let not the darkness claim its prize,
For every end brings new sunrise.
In whispered winds, their voices blend,
A eulogy for light transcends.

So raise your eyes to heavens wide,
In gratitude, let love abide.
For every star that dims its hue,
Reminds us all of love so true.

Beneath the Cloak of Nightingale's Song

In the stillness, whispers rise,
A melody that soars and flies.
The stars align with sacred grace,
Beneath the night, we find our place.

Hearts entwined in soft embrace,
The light of faith, a gentle trace.
Each note a prayer, a love divine,
In nightingale's song, we intertwine.

Through shadows deep, we search for peace,
In every sorrow, find release.
The cloak of night, a holy shroud,
In silence sweet, we sing aloud.

With every breath, a sacred sigh,
We rise as one, to touch the sky.
In timeless tune, forever strong,
We dance within the nightingale's song.

The Lent of Solitude

In the desert of our hearts,
A quiet voice, the journey starts.
With each tear, a lesson learned,
In solitude, our souls are turned.

Forsaken paths may seem so long,
Yet in this trial, we grow strong.
Each moment speaks of sacrifice,
A call to rise beyond the vice.

Amid the stillness, spirits mend,
In solitary, we transcend.
A whisper crescent moon imparts,
Embraced within, a journey charts.

From ashes found, new life ascends,
In depths of silence, light extends.
The Lent of Solitude, a grace,
In solitude, we find our place.

Sanctified by the Abyss

In shadows deep, the spirit yearns,
Through trials fierce, a heart discerns.
From depths of woe, a peace restored,
In the abyss, our faith is poured.

Sanctuary in the dark revealed,
A promise kept, our wounds are healed.
Each tear a testament of strength,
In vast abyss, we find our length.

With every heartbeat, grace bestowed,
Through barren lands, our spirits strode.
In sacred void, our souls enhance,
Within the depths, we find our dance.

Sanctified by trials wrought,
In arduous paths, the battle fought.
The abyss, a cradle of rebirth,
In darkness, we find our worth.

Blessed Are Those Who Weep

In sorrow's grip, the spirit bends,
Yet with each tear, a love transcends.
For every heart that breaks in pain,
A blessing blooms, like gentle rain.

The weeping eyes see truths unfold,
In every story, hope is told.
Through trials faced, our souls ignite,
In darkest hours, we seek the light.

To weep is to embrace the soul,
In every heartache, find the whole.
Blessed are those who bear the load,
In brokenness, the path is road.

With heavy hearts, we search for grace,
In tears, the tender love we trace.
Each drop a seed of faith we sow,
In weeping's depth, true love will grow.

Prophecies of New Dawn

Whispers of light on the horizon,
Guiding the souls lost in the night.
Truths unfold in the early morning,
Awakening hope, a glorious sight.

Mountains bow, and oceans rise,
In harmony, nature sings anew.
Every heartbeat echoes with promise,
The dawn of grace, shining through.

Tears of the past wash away,
In the glow of the shining sun.
A tapestry woven with faith,
Together, we embrace what's begun.

Angels dance in the golden rays,
Calling forth the weary and meek.
A symphony of life rejoices,
In every prayer that we speak.

True love reigns where fear once dwelled,
Filling our spirits with pure delight.
Under the watch of sacred skies,
New beginnings take flight tonight.

Testaments of Forgotten Love

In the silence of ancient hearts,
Echoes of warmth linger still.
Whispers of promises unbroken,
Captured in time, forever will.

Faded letters lie in the dust,
Words of longing, passion's trace.
Each syllable a gentle reminder,
Of a love that transcends time and space.

Stars in the night hold our secrets,
Guiding our dreams to realms divine.
A tapestry woven with memories,
In the heart's sanctuary they shine.

Though miles may keep us apart,
Faith connects the threads of our souls.
In every heartbeat, I feel you near,
Love everlasting, it consoles.

Testaments written in starlight,
Reminders of what once was ours.
In the quiet, I still hear your voice,
A love that outshines the brightest stars.

Sanctuary of the Heart's Weeping

In the shadows, the heart is found,
Battling storms that rage within.
Cries lifted to the heavens high,
Seeking solace where love has been.

Every tear a sacred offering,
A testament of trials faced.
In the silence, the spirit strengthens,
Embracing grief, yet filled with grace.

The sanctuary holds all our fears,
Walls of compassion, comforted space.
Here, our burdens are gently lifted,
In the light, sorrows find their place.

Whispers of hope breathe through the pain,
Each heartbeat a promise renewed.
In the warmth of divine acceptance,
Hearts mend, and love is imbued.

Together we rise from the ashes,
Strong like the roots of a towering tree.
In this sanctuary, we find rebirth,
The heart's weeping sets our spirits free.

The Spirit's Resurgence

In the stillness, the Spirit breathes,
Igniting flames of faith once more.
Filling the void with sacred whispers,
Guiding our path to the open door.

In shadows cast by doubt and fear,
A light ignites, dispelling night.
Renewed in purpose, hearts awaken,
To the call of love's radiant light.

Mountains crumble, chains are broken,
In the presence of grace, we soar.
Transcending limits of earthly bounds,
Our spirits dance on heaven's floor.

The journey unfolds, rich with meaning,
Every step a testament of soul.
Boundless joy in moments fleeting,
As we embrace what makes us whole.

Together we chase the dawn's promise,
In unity, hearts become one.
The Spirit's resurgence ignites us,
Blessed by the power of the sun.

The Crossroads of Forgiveness

In shadows cast by pain we stand,
Two paths diverge upon the land.
One leads to love, the other strife,
Choose the road that grants us life.

Whispers echo on the breeze,
A gentle call, a simple tease.
Forgiveness blooms in tender hearts,
A healing touch that never parts.

With open arms we face the storm,
In grace we find our spirits warm.
Let go of burdens, heavy chains,
In light of peace, the spirit gains.

Through trials long, we walk this way,
The dawn of hope paints night to day.
For in the wounds, the light shall gleam,
Forgiveness flows, a sacred stream.

At crossroads meet, let silence reign,
In stillness find the joy in pain.
With every breath we share our song,
In unity, we all belong.

Solace in the Sacred Void

In silence deep, where shadows fade,
The heart finds peace, a quiet glade.
In sacred void, our spirits soar,
Embracing all, we seek for more.

A whisper soft, the soul's embrace,
In solitude, we find our place.
The emptiness, a canvas wide,
Where love and grace can safely hide.

With every breath, we breathe the light,
In darkness deep, we find our sight.
The sacred void, a tender birth,
Where echoes of creation mirth.

In moments hushed, we feel the call,
To rise above, to never fall.
For in the still, our truth is found,
In every heartbeat, love abound.

So let us dwell in sacred space,
Where time stands still, and souls embrace.
In unity, we find our song,
In the void, we all belong.

Translations of a Broken Heart

From shards of sorrow, beauty blooms,
In brokenness, the spirit grooms.
The heart, a vessel, cracked and worn,
Yet in the pain, new life is born.

Every tear, a story told,
In softest hues, the heart unfolds.
Translations speak in tender sighs,
Of love lost deep, yet hope still flies.

Within the ache, a truth reveals,
In vulnerability, the heart heals.
Resilience found in shadows cast,
Through every trial, we rise at last.

Let every scar become a tale,
A testament where we prevail.
For broken hearts can learn to sing,
In every loss, a new hope brings.

So gather close, O souls in pain,
In translations, find joy in rain.
Together here, we mend and start,
In every beat, a sacred heart.

The Prophet's Crescent

In crescent light, the prophet speaks,
With wisdom deep and truth that seeks.
A guiding star through darkest night,
In every word, a spark of light.

Among the lost, his voice will soar,
A call to love, to seek for more.
He walks the path of heart and soul,
A bridge that mends, a sacred goal.

In every tear, his heart he gives,
The wounded learn, the spirit lives.
A prophet's grace in every sigh,
To lift the weak and help them fly.

With open hands, he scatters seeds,
Of hope and faith in wandering needs.
Crescent moon, a gentle guide,
Together we, in warmth abide.

So let us hear the prophet's call,
In unity, we rise, not fall.
For in his words, the truth is found,
In every heart, where love is crowned.

Pilgrimage of the Lost

In shadows deep, we wander far,
Seeking light, a distant star.
Our hearts are heavy, spirits torn,
Yet hope ignites, a new dawn born.

With each step, we shed our fears,
In silent prayers, we shed our tears.
The path is long, the night is cold,
But faith will guide, and love enfolds.

O weary soul, find strength anew,
In every trial, His love breaks through.
For in our lostness, we will find,
A greater truth, divinely kind.

Through valleys low, and mountains high,
We lift our gaze, and seek the sky.
Each soul adrift, a sacred quest,
In journey's end, we find our rest.

So onward tread, through pain and strife,
In search of grace, the breath of life.
The pilgrimage leads us homeward bound,
Where lost and found in Him are crowned.

Gethsemane of the Forsaken

In shadows deep, a garden sighs,
Beneath the weight, the heart replies.
Forsaken souls, in silence stand,
With trembling hearts and outstretched hands.

Each whispered prayer, a mournful plea,
In solitude, we seek to be.
With bitter tears we water ground,
In hope's embrace, salvation found.

The weight of thorns, the price we pay,
In darkest night, we find our way.
In sorrow's grip, we kneel and plead,
For grace to bloom, a sacred seed.

Gethsemane calls, a sacred space,
Where faith and doubt together grace.
Forsaken yet, we rise anew,
Through trials faced, our spirit grew.

In unity, we bear our pain,
Through every loss, love will remain.
With every heartbeat, courage speaks,
In Gethsemane, the spirit seeks.

Hymnal Whispers of Release

In gentle tones, the hymns arise,
Soft melodies, beneath the skies.
They call the weary, the broken hearts,
To find the peace that love imparts.

With every note, a burden lifts,
In sacred sound, we find our gifts.
The whispers echo, all around,
In harmony, our souls are found.

Release the chains that bind the past,
In soaring songs, our spirits cast.
Embrace the light, let shadows flee,
In hymnal whispers, we are free.

With voices raised, we sing our truth,
In every line, there's hope and youth.
A symphony of hearts combined,
In love's embrace, we're redefined.

So join the choir, let your soul soar,
In every refrain, forevermore.
For in this song, we find our place,
In hymnal whispers, we find grace.

The Crossroads of Healing

At the crossroads, where spirits meet,
In healing hands, we find our feet.
With every choice that bids us stay,
A path of grace lights up the way.

Through whispered prayers, the wounded rise,
In sacred light, despair defies.
Each step we take, one heart at a time,
In unity, we rise and climb.

The journey long, but love must bear,
The weight of sorrow, the sound of prayer.
With courage bold, we face the night,
At the crossroads, we seek the light.

For in our wounds, the truth we find,
In brokenness, the heart's aligned.
A tapestry of hope we weave,
In healing grace, we can believe.

So come, dear soul, to where we stand,
At the crossroads, hand in hand.
Together bound, in love we heal,
In faith's embrace, our hope is real.

The Light Within the Lament

In shadows deep, the spirits soar,
With whispers soft, they plead for more.
Each tear a prayer, each sigh a song,
In darkness find where we belong.

The heartache glows, a silent flame,
Lighting paths where once was shame.
In sacred echoes, hope's refrain,
The light within our grief remains.

From sorrow's grasp, our souls take flight,
To seek the dawn, to find the light.
Embrace the pain, let it be known,
In every loss, we are not alone.

With every whisper of the night,
We rise again to greet the light.
Within the lament, there's strength to find,
A journey carved by the divine.

So let us sing through tears and fears,
Transform our loss into light that clears.
The candle burns, a beacon bright,
The light within, our greatest fight.

Monuments of the Forsaken

In silence they stand, the stones of pain,
Monuments speaking of love and disdain.
Forgotten whispers in the wind's caress,
Echoes of lives dressed in sorrow's dress.

Each name engraved, a tale untold,
In hallowed ground, we find the bold.
Remember the lost, their stories sung,
In sacred spaces, forever young.

We gather in prayer, hearts intertwined,
In grief we find the ties that bind.
Each monument a testament bright,
To lives once lived, now bathed in light.

Forsaken no more, their spirits rise,
As we honor the past, through loving eyes.
In unity we stand, strong and proud,
For the forsaken souls, we speak aloud.

Their dreams we carry, their hopes we bear,
In every step, we find them there.
Monuments of love, faith will renew,
In remembrance, our spirits pursue.

The Sacrifice of Remembering

In quiet moments, memories dwell,
The sacrifice of love, a sacred spell.
In every heartbeat, stories thread,
A tapestry woven by those who fled.

We keep their voices, alive in prayer,
The strength we find, a bond we share.
For in our hearts, they still reside,
Their legacy, our faithful guide.

Through tears we learn, through loss we gain,
Embracing sorrow, we rise again.
Each memory sparked, a fire within,
In remembering, a new dawn begins.

With every prayer, we honor the past,
The sacrifice of love, forever vast.
In shadows cast by fading light,
We pledge to keep their dreams in sight.

So let us forge a path anew,
With gratitude for all they knew.
In the sacrifice, their love we cling,
In every heartbeat, their voices sing.

Dusk Before the Dawn

In twilight's grasp, hope softly gleams,
Between the shadows, whispers of dreams.
Each sorrow felt, a lesson learned,
In darkest times, our spirits burned.

The dusk may linger, but light will find,
The hidden corners of heart and mind.
Through trials faced with faithful grace,
The dawn will break, in a warm embrace.

So let us rise, our eyes anew,
Embracing change, the skies so blue.
The dawn approaches, fierce and bright,
In every shadow, embers of light.

The night may test, but we hold strong,
In unity, we will belong.
For every dawn brings endless chance,
A sacred rhythm, a timeless dance.

With faith as guide, we journey on,
Through dusk and dark, till the breaking dawn.
In every moment, our hearts entwined,
We lift our voices, love aligned.

The Celestial Harvest of Heartache

In fields where shadows softly dwell,
The soul reaps sorrow, woven well.
Each tear a seed, each sigh a prayer,
In grief's embrace, we find our share.

The heavens watch, their gaze so near,
As heartache blooms, the silence clear.
With every loss, the spirit grows,
In darkness deep, the light still glows.

From yearning's depth, a melody,
Transcends the pain, and sets us free.
In brokenness, a strength is found,
In every crack, the grace abound.

There lies a beauty in the scars,
A testament beneath the stars.
For every wound, a lesson learned,
In love's harsh fire, the heart is turned.

So let us gather sorrow's yield,
With faith as our steadfast shield.
In heartache's harvest, seeds will sprout,
Towards joy's horizon, we'll reach out.

Chronicles of a Pilgrim's Soliloquy

Upon this path, my feet do roam,
In search of solace, far from home.
The whispers guide, the echoes call,
A sacred journey, steeped in thrall.

Each step I take, a tale unfolds,
In quiet nights, the truth beholds.
The stars above, my faithful light,
In shadows deep, they banish night.

Through valleys low and mountains high,
I lift my gaze to the open sky.
With every heartache, wisdom sighs,
In solitude, my spirit flies.

The road unknown, I walk with grace,
In trials faced, I find my place.
With every breath, a prayer is sent,
In pilgrimage, my soul is bent.

Each step, a chronicle of old,
Of fears embraced, and faith retold.
The pilgrimage shall never cease,
For in each moment, I find peace.

Blessings in the Ruins of Affection

In crumbled walls where love once stood,
The echoes whisper, soft and good.
Each broken shard tells tales of grace,
In ruins deep, we find our place.

The ashes bear a gentle touch,
Reminding hearts, we care so much.
In every loss, a blessing sown,
In what was lost, we are not alone.

Through tangled vines, affection grows,
In fractured light, the beauty shows.
What once was broken, now made whole,
In love's embrace, we find our soul.

The memories linger, sweet and bright,
In shadows cast, love leads to light.
From ruin's depth, a seed will rise,
In every tear, the truth complies.

So let us cherish what remains,
In love's ruins, no heart in chains.
For every ending, a new start,
In blessings found, we mend the heart.

The Light Beyond the Broken Way

In fractured paths, where shadows lay,
There shines a light to guide the way.
A beacon calls through darkest nights,
In broken dreams, the heart ignites.

The journey leads through pain and strife,
Yet in each stumble, there's new life.
With faith as anchor, hope we find,
In every tear, the heart aligned.

Beyond the hurt, the dawn will break,
A promise held, no soul forsake.
Through trials faced, the spirit soars,
In shattered dreams, the soul restores.

The light within, forever glows,
In deepest valleys, love bestows.
With every falter, we are blessed,
In brokenness, we find our rest.

So journey forth, though darkness calls,
For after storms, the sunlight falls.
In shattered ways, our hearts will say,
There's light and love beyond the fray.

The Divine Unraveling of Attachments

In silence, we ponder the bonds that we hold,
Like threads that entwine in a tapestry bold.
Yet faith whispers softly, 'Let go of the chains,'
For in letting go, true freedom remains.

The heart learns to dance in the light of release,
Embracing the calm where the soul finds its peace.
With courage, we sever the ties that ensnare,
And rise like the dawn, in the warmth of His care.

The struggle unravels, revealing the grace,
That blossoms anew in a sacred space.
Each tear that we shed becomes fertile ground,
Where love found in trust is eternally bound.

Through trials and lessons, our spirits take flight,
In the depths of the darkness, we uncover the light.
With each step we take, the path becomes clear,
As we walk with the One who is ever so near.

No longer confined by the fears we then knew,
In the embrace of divinity, we start anew.
For in the dissolving of ego's tight grip,
We find that the soul is a limitless ship.

Manifestation of Grace from Shadows

In the stillness of night, when the stars softly gleam,
A whisper of grace flows like a soothing dream.
From shadows we rise, as the dawn breaks the dark,
Embracing the light, we ignite a new spark.

Within every silence, a promise is sown,
That in depths of despair, we are never alone.
With faith like a river, we let it all stream,
Transforming the shadows into radiant beams.

The heart can unlock what was once locked away,
As love pours forth with the light of the day.
In surrender, we find a divine kind of grace,
Emerging anew in a sacred embrace.

Each struggle a stepping stone leading us home,
To a place where together we shall freely roam.
With gratitude tender, we thank every trial,
For each one has shaped us, transforming our smile.

The tapestry woven with threads of our tears,
Is colored with wisdom, a gift through the years.
In shadows we once wandered, now graciously bloom,
Life's beauty unveiled in its brightest costume.

The Pilgrimage of the Wandering Spirit

We journey through valleys, where footsteps are few,
With hearts full of longing, we seek to be true.
The path may be winding, the skies ever gray,
But a light calls us onward, guiding our way.

Each mountain we climb brings us closer to peace,
As the burdens we carry gently begin to cease.
In every encounter, a lesson unfolds,
With stories of courage and faith yet untold.

The spirit, a wanderer, knows no bounds,
Finding grace in the forests, where wisdom abounds.
In the whispers of nature, a voice calls us near,
Reminding us softly that love conquers fear.

Through rivers and storms, we gather our strength,
Designing our journey with love as the length.
For each step we take is a prayer to the skies,
An act of devotion, where our true self lies.

So, let us keep wandering, with faith as our guide,
Embracing each moment, with our hearts open wide.
Though the pilgrimage may take us far and away,
We're nourished by love, come what may.

Retrieving Hope from Fractured Dreams

In the ashes of dreams that once brightly shone,
We gather the pieces, though hope feels alone.
For every decline, there's a rise that appears,
Reminding us softly that love conquers fears.

With hands outstretched wide, we collect what is lost,
Embracing the journey, no matter the cost.
In shadows of doubt, where despair starts to creep,
A flicker of promise ignites from the deep.

The heart learns the art of transforming the pain,
Creating a pathway through life's fierce rain.
In the healing of scars, new visions arise,
Drawing strength from the struggle, a gift in disguise.

So let us reclaim what was thought to be gone,
With courage, let's dance to the beat of our song.
For in every fracture, there's beauty to find,
A tapestry woven with threads that bind.

Hope whispers gently, 'You are never alone,'
As we gather our dreams and make them our own.
With faith ever steadfast, we rise from the dust,
Reviving our spirits, reborn from the rust.

Celestial Clarity in Broken Promises

In shadows cast by promises slight,
The stars still shine, a guiding light.
With every vow that fades away,
Hope blossoms anew at break of day.

Each tear we shed upon the stone,
Bears witness to the seeds we've sown.
In broken trust we find our grace,
A dance of sorrow in this sacred space.

For even when the night seems long,
The soul within begins to song.
In clarity, our hearts ignite,
Transforming pain to purest light.

So let the heavens weep and moan,
For in our trials, we are not alone.
The celestial map, it draws us near,
To love reborn, beyond the fear.

In each tear's fall, a promise kept,
For every soul, a love adept.
With open arms, we greet the dawn,
In celestial realms, our faith is drawn.

Ascetic Love's Quiet Rebirth

In silence, where the heart doth dwell,
Ascetic love weaves its gentle spell.
With empty hands and open sights,
We seek the warmth of inner lights.

Each whispered prayer, a seed bestowed,
In barren lands, true love is sowed.
With every sacrifice we make,
The spirit soars, a life awake.

Through trials faced in solitude,
We find the path, our hearts renewed.
Like phoenix rising from the ash,
In quiet moments, passions clash.

As dawn unveils the veil of night,
The soul is brimmed with pure delight.
Ascetic love, a sacred thread,
In this rebirth, our spirits wed.

So let us cherish what we forsake,
In every choice, our heart's own stake.
With humble hearts, we seek the grace,
Of ascetic love in sacred space.

Sacred Whispers in the Void

In the silence of the starless sky,
Sacred whispers gently sigh.
Through the void where shadows creep,
The truth awakens from its sleep.

In every echo of despair,
The sacred speaks, a truth laid bare.
With open hearts to hear the call,
We find the strength to rise, not fall.

From nothingness, the light does bloom,
In the dark, dispelling gloom.
Each whisper carries hope anew,
In sacred bonds, we find our due.

In trials faced, we seek the word,
The silent call, deeply heard.
Through endless void, the spirit flies,
In sacred whispers, our soul ties.

For in the stillness, love persists,
Through every shadow, our heart insists.
Sacred whispers, our guiding flame,
In the void, we rise, unashamed.

Lamentation's Sacred Fire

In lamentation, we find our grace,
A sacred fire in this dark space.
Each tear a candle, brightly burns,
Through pain and sorrow, the spirit learns.

In the embers of our broken dreams,
We find the strength, or so it seems.
A dance of anguish in twilight's glow,
From ashes, we rise; our hearts bestow.

Through nights of loss, we brave the storm,
In sacred fire, our hearts transform.
With every cry that pierces night,
We forge a path, embrace the light.

Lamentation's song, a bittersweet tune,
In every shadow, love will bloom.
The sacred fire, a guiding spark,
It lights our way through the dismal dark.

So let us gather 'round the flame,
In unity, we call each name.
For in our sorrow, we shall find,
The sacred fire, love intertwined.

The Serene Stillness

In the quiet, hearts do speak,
Where whispers of the soul do seek.
A gentle breeze through the trees,
Brings peace and solace, like a soft tease.

Mountains watch with ancient grace,
As time unfolds its sacred space.
In stillness, we find the light,
Guiding us through the darkest night.

Rivers flow with purpose pure,
Their secrets deep, their paths sure.
Nature sings a soothing hymn,
In harmony, our fears grow dim.

Stars above, like candles bright,
Illuminating the sacred night.
In solitude, our spirits soar,
Finding strength forevermore.

Let the stillness wrap us whole,
Embracing the depths of soul to soul.
In every moment, grace distills,
In the serene, eternal thrills.

The Serpent and the Sacred

In shadows lurks the wise old serpent,
Woven truths in a twisted current.
He guards the secrets of the night,
With scales that shimmer, a mystical sight.

Beneath the branches, wisdom reigns,
A dance of life amid the rains.
In every coil, a story lies,
Of creation's breath and ancient skies.

Sacred ground where we tread,
With every step, the past is wed.
In unity, the light does gleam,
As hope emerges from the dream.

The serpent whispers ancient lore,
Of battles fought, of love and more.
In his eyes, the truth we find,
A path to heal, to intertwine.

In reverence, we weave the thread,
Linking heart to heart, the light is spread.
The sacred dance, we join as one,
In the eternal cycle of the sun.

The Alchemy of Abandonment

In letting go, we find our wings,
A freedom that the spirit sings.
Each heavy burden falls away,
Releasing chains that led astray.

Through the ashes, new life flows,
Transforming trials, where love still grows.
In surrender, we rise anew,
With open hearts, our spirits view.

Like leaves that fall in autumn's grace,
We trust the earth, our rightful place.
In loss, there's beauty yet unseen,
The alchemy where we redeem.

Embrace the tears, the bitter cry,
In those moments, we learn to fly.
Transcending pain, we find our worth,
Creating gold from the depths of earth.

A journey shaped by faith and light,
Awakening souls to inner sight.
In abandonment, we find our truth,
A precious gift, the bloom of youth.

Arising in the Solitary

In solitude, a voice resounds,
Within the heart, the truth abounds.
In quiet moments, wisdom wakes,
A sacred bond that never breaks.

The path ahead, though lone and bare,
Becomes a canvas, bright and fair.
In stillness, dreams begin to form,
A guiding star, a sacred norm.

The echoes of the past remind,
That in retreat, we seek to find.
A deeper sense of grace and peace,
In silent strength, our fears release.

Each breath a prayer, each thought a song,
In solitude, we all belong.
With every step, we honor fate,
Embracing love, we rise elate.

So let us celebrate this time,
A sacred rhythm, a sacred rhyme.
In solitary, hearts entwine,
A symphony of the divine.

Seraphic Solitude

In quietude, the soul takes flight,
Amidst the whispers of the night.
Angelic voices softly sing,
Of peace and hope that solitude brings.

In stillness found, the heart reveals,
The grace, the truth, the love it feels.
Each moment blessed, a sacred space,
To meet the light, to seek His face.

A journey deep within the soul,
Where faith and spirit become whole.
The aloneness, a divine retreat,
In solitude, we find our seat.

With every prayer, a gentle sigh,
A lifting heart, a longing high.
Beneath the stars, the shadows fade,
In silence pure, our lives are laid.

Thus in this vast eternity,
We find our seraphic clarity.
In the embrace of holy night,
Solitude becomes our guiding light.

Resilient Faith in Despair

When darkened skies begin to fall,
And shadows stretch, they seem so tall.
In depths of anguish, hearts may break,
Yet steadfast faith, we shall not shake.

Through trials fierce, the spirit fights,
In darkness, we behold the lights.
Each tear a prayer, each sigh a song,
In hope, through faith, we will belong.

The tempest rages, winds may howl,
Yet still we rise, our faith, a prowl.
For every storm that seeks to claim,
Our souls ignite, we call His name.

From ashes born, the heart anew,
In every struggle, courage grew.
Resilience shines—a holy stance,
Through faith's embrace, we find our chance.

So let us walk, though shadows cast,
Knowing that trials, they too shall pass.
In every pain, a purpose clear,
Resilient faith shall persevere.

A Covenant with Solitude

In quiet moments, whispers flow,
The heart concedes, the spirit knows.
A covenant forged in peace divine,
In solitude, our souls entwine.

We seek the depth of silence pure,
In stillness found, our hearts endure.
The sacred bond, an oath of grace,
With every breath, we seek His face.

Through loneliness, a strength we gain,
In quietude, the love remains.
Embracing solitude's sweet call,
In sacred space, we rise, we fall.

For here the spirit learns to soar,
In silent hours, we seek for more.
A trust so deep, forever bound,
In solitude, His grace is found.

Each hour alone, a gift bestowed,
On paths of faith, our courage flowed.
A covenant made, a heart set free,
In solitude, we come to see.

The Light After the Veil

Through shadows deep, the soul will tread,
On paths unknown, where fears are fed.
Yet in the darkness, hope prevails,
We yearn to see the light that quails.

Beyond the veil, a promise lies,
A dawn reborn, a clear blue sky.
With every tear, a prayer ascends,
The heart believes, the spirit mends.

In trials faced, the truth exposed,
The greatest love, our hearts enclosed.
For in the silence, whispers call,
The light will shine, it conquers all.

Each moment grieved, each burden borne,
With heavy heart, our hope's reborn.
The light breaks through, a gentle grace,
Beyond the veil, we'll find our place.

So, lift your gaze, embrace the flame,
For light shall guide, we're not the same.
From darkness deep to dawn so bright,
We stand in faith, embrace the light.

Milton Keynes UK
Ingram Content Group UK Ltd.
UKHW022121021224
451618UK00039B/127